WHAT YOU LEAVE BEHIND

What You Leave Behind

Mahendra Solanki

BLACKWATER
P R E S S

First Published in United Kingdom in 1996
by
Blackwater Press
17 Holbrook Road, Leicester LE2 3LG
England

Printed in England by
Leighton Printing Company
London N7 8DH

British Library Cataloguing in Publication Data

Solanki, Mahendra, 1956
    What You Leave Behind
    1. English poetry - 20th century
    1. Title
    821.9'14

ISBN 0 9528557 0 4

for

Hilary Frances
Hannah Bhavani
Ansuya Isabella

POSSESSIONS

If I was to flee from you, I had to flee from the family as well, even from mother.

Franz Kafka, *Letter to his father*

BAPUJI

It was the sound at first
A break in the dark
And the white wafer of light
At your feet by the door
That startles to mind
What fears I had then as a child.

      Mistaking distance for protection
      (As some mistake darkness for shelter)
      I imagined a hundred miles to be far enough
      From duty and obligation; in another city
      Covering tracks, side-stepping informers,
      I talked you away, thinking myself safe.

But on long nights in rented rooms
I still hear footsteps - yours,
Yours, come to haunt me
Back to your future.

A MOTHER'S ADVICE

Remember, wherever you live,
Always guard your keys.

They have taken away my shoes,
They have taken away my clothes.

Stay in command of your senses;
Think before you speak.

Remember men at work
Are plotting behind you.

As your brothers get older
There is trouble ahead.

Keep a watchful eye on your brothers working,
Keep a watchful eye on your sisters.

But only meet your brothers and sisters
As strangers at a distance.

You cannot call your brother-in-law your father.
Keep an eye on your wife also.

Only by being on guard
Will you win on a point.

When they offer to put you up,
Refuse their company in bed.
Both of them will take away your strength.
Step-mothers and step-fathers are not relations.

Remember that.
Keep your emotions in check.

ELDEST SON

My second child, but my eldest son,
My reason against despair,
                            A wedge
In the door, letting in light.

When you left, without explaining,
I knew you would, like a son, return.

I prayed each day and cried
Your brothers and sisters to sleep.

More precious to me than my own life,
How can you now choose to live apart?

Living in this kitchen, hearing only voices,
Hurts more than your father's blows.

Your leaving, without warning,
Banged shut my life.

POSSESSION

Since Manu left
She's come in
To eat away my heart.

Snake   She's come in
Through the blouse I wear.

How can I name her? Even God
weeps at hearing her name.

Comb my hair? It's the hair
she has grabbed me by.
I used to wash and pray
once, she won't let me now.
She's taking my life.

What has she taught you?
Why do you go to her to learn?

She holds me by my ankle.
She holds my tongue from speaking.

I will not leave you
I will remain with you
As long as you're in this room.
What are you offering those prayers for?"

Those witches honour *Mataji*
To learn by, possessing her.
Doesn't your brain work?
Can't you see?

How can you?
Dharam kar.

16

Being your father's wife,
She dresses, eats and travels;
Even then she asks your
Sister to send her more.

If she's become your mother,
She should do so by right.

You cannot see anything
How can you see anything?
She keeps you happy now,
It's only after they've taken my life
Will she take her revenge.

He has taken up with those *vasayas*.
They want to scatter my children.

Do you hear me?

ALWAYS THERE

Your idea for keeping us safe
is for us all to sleep together,
huddled against your ghosts
in a room paid for in advance.

You would keep us fed;
cooker balanced in the corner,
food stored in the oven.

We would stay indoors.
School, work and love,
unnecessary distractions.

We would never grow old.
Strangers, you tell us,
would only lie.

MIRROR

An empty bed faces me
now that she has gone

I remember her nightly vigils
her constant talk

Now that she has gone
an empty bed faces me

A young man's face
now stares at me in silence.

HOMECOMING

As the train startles forward
she jolts backwards, dazed
to a seat opposite me.

We stare blankly, both into
a book where the line is constant,
both on a long journey that
I know does not take me home.

                        Back
to a mother and child
in a town where
no roads meet.

A WAIT AS LONG AS A TRAIN

I have been waiting for you all my life,
A wait that seemed as long
As the train that brought you here.
How can I tell you
                                You're too late?
Even though I chant your name
Like an old mantra through the day,
And dial your number in my head.

WHAT YOU LEFT BEHIND

I have always dodged you and hidden from you, in my room, among my books, with crazy friends, or with extravagant ideas. I have never talked to you frankly, I have never come to you...

Franz Kafka, *Letter to his father*

DETAIL

Death is a cliché

Flames always leap
Water always flows
Tears always stream
Questions remain unasked
Death is a full stop.
It is the detail that shocks:

Your skin with nails intact
Dropped outside the drain
By the Council men in their haste.

BAG

There was a complicated physical side to the ceremony, as with
so many Hindu ceremonies: knowing where on the altar to put
the sacrificial flowers, knowing how to sing the verses and
when, knowing how and when and where to pour various
substances: the whole mechanical side of priesthood.
V.S.Naipaul, *The Enigma of Arrival*

I spread out new clothes
(bought from stores you avoided
 insisting out of a meanness, on making do):
a suit, a vest, a shirt, a tie and
pants over a bag in which your body lies.

You are spared death's grandeur;
no lying in state with rouged cheeks.
Your brother asks an attendant,
"Couldn't you pretty him up a little?"

> *Avoiding touch, I brush you gently*
> *then out of curiosity, prod you hard,*
> *hard against a zipped up bag,*
> *hard against the bone.*

> *I want to see you again*
> *whole naked to the bone*
> *charred black by the cold.*

I walk around you
laying out objects as rehearsed with aunts
guessing at a sequence of order.
I empty phials of perfume,
                              arrange flower petals,
balance a chip of metal by your head -
it should be in your mouth.

I confess to a tenderness
                    against your hardened bones.
An old anger long dissipated.

What remains still is a fear
as fixed as the scowl on your face.
As real as the stench you left behind.

IN A JAR

I collect you in a jar.

I always imagined it would be ornamental,
                                        like a trophy.
It is plastic and weighs more than
its square shape suggests.

I lower you gently into the boot of the car, you in
a plastic jar propped against plastic bags full of offerings.

I have a thud in my head
as dull as the brown of the jar.
Shri Ram jaya Ram jaya jaya Ram.
I am driven to discard your remains in running water.

> *I imagine all your hardened*
> *edges made smooth;*
> *a life-time's harshness*
> *burnt clean by fire.*

I take off my shoes and in socks
                              on the Severn's edge
float a clay pot and *paan* leaves.

                    I plop balls of flour -
there are so many they begin to gather around my feet;
landlocked by flowers, rice, cotton threads and god knows what.
Worried that all this will not move,
                        (I am aware of people staring),
I almost topple into the river as I aim
throws as far as my stiff neck allows.

I hold you squat in my hands,
open the cap and spill you out.

Solemnly at first, then with a final gush
I swill you out with the water;
muttering a request for peace
as you go with the river
                        pulled down into the sea.

TRADEMARK

This woman tells me how you would arrive late
unannounced, and on not finding a cooked meal
kick her as she lay rolled up on a stone floor;

of how you have thrown her small child
across an open floor against a bare wall;

of how you have used whatever came to hand to harm;
of how you built a garden at the back to stop
her five children from playing outside;

of how you have bolted all windows and each door;
of how you have ordered her to stay indoors.

You have maimed and hurt across three continents,
abused all those who came into your care.

> *If you were still alive*
> *I may yet roll fear into a fist*
> *and beat my rage out of you.*

Men leave behind some acts of kindness
in a life lived, for the most part, shabbily.

You have left behind cowering children
and silent women staring in shuttered rooms;
frightened by their own helplessness
and an indelible trademark: a fist, a boot.

STILL

I have stared in mirrors
seen you often

seen in that arched smile
                    your fat grin

seen in those bulged cheeks
                    your full face

A SLIGHT BREEZE

These are the lives you left behind:
aunt, uncle, nephews and nieces,
these I seek, those that claim kinship;
none that I can call my own.

Your life, with secret selves
I untangle from the man.
Your dying, a slight breeze, changes little:
a maze of names and places,
of relations and villages, of rights and wrongs.

I am a stranger in your land,
as I was when you were alive.
Your brother and sister plot behind me:
there are pacts to keep me out.

A WING

A great aunt uncovers a brass plate
to read in the smear of white flour
(spread on the day of your cremation)
the means by which you left this life.

She pauses, as I strain in the circle
of women, hoping to see ...
A plane, a car, a horse-drawn chariot
Like Surya's, rising like a flower?

My great aunt, a surviving custodian of customs,
with owl white hair, warm with white fur,
sits in the centre, *"It is hard to say ...*
but wait ... this looks like the wing of an aeroplane."
The circle flaps to reassure her and all will a plane
in the spread of white now flecked with grey.

I see only a wing and want almost to jeer;
but it *is* hard to say how you went.
You have been gone so long, so much
of you had seeped through;
so much of you a rubberised lava
on the floor of your resting place.

Even if you have not yet departed,
seeped into lives scarred by your shadow,
I cannot will you a one-way ticket
on an aeroplane with just one wing.

ONE KNOCK DOWN OR TWO SUBMISSIONS

You wanted me to be a wrestler.
For a while you encouraged me to eat
meat, drink milk and exercise
on a set of chest expanders.

You cajoled my sister, a year older,
but a lot stronger, to wrestle with me.
She usually won, much to your pleasure.
You grew disappointed at what I could do.

You knew I liked reading, knowing little
of why, or how reading removed me from you.
Not able to read English yourself,
you made me read aloud titles of Hindi films
in English from leaflets posted through the door.
When the sounds I made did not match yours,
you scorned and your displeasure grew.

I now watch wrestling on television with my daughter.
We delight at the sight of over the top
stunts of wrestlers in sequins or at a leotarded
brute wielding a plank of wood in the ring.
I do not know if you would have approved of this:
this showing off or laying bare the performer's art.

Learning late that you made all the rules
before the start, mocks the final bell.

EXERCISES IN TRUST

from mourning into morning

George Barker, *To My Mother*

"If it be love indeed, tell me how much"

for Hannah

You say, "I don't love you,"
pinching your forefinger and thumb,
your hand a small fish's head,
"even *this* much."

Arching both arms out, you say,
your arms now a seagull's wings,
"I love David *that* much"

At five you think of love
as a measuring rod;
each notch a fist
to use as a bargaining tool.

On your first birthday, I thought
of time as a measure of love:
a life-time of love a year old;
"I'll love you for ever" held at the water's edge.

You and I stand on a shoreline.
We are bound by what we hear and say.
Stones sink like hopes.

How can I gauge the depth
of the sea we throw pebbles in?

BLINDFOLD:
EXERCISES IN TRUST

for Catherine Byron

(i)

I taught him to read signs
of what to trust
                    my hands
a guide for his eyes

How a landscape can deceive
how a lake
                    so much like a moon
can drown a shadow

(ii)

You taste of wet grass
your body is bruised like a wall
your hands are covered by bark

your fingers are branches
                    numb to my touch

(iii)

I trusted you when you
took away my eyes

I walked in your shadow
as you led me through moonlight

I crawled on all fours
as you stood over me

I drank from a broken tap
as you turned on the hose

I cut myself falling
as you took away my hand

I waited for you to come
as you left me drowning in a pool

      (iv)
I waited for you to hold me
for your body
          a frame of clothes
to break my fall

      (v)
Is it you or is it them
who walk away from me?

HAIKU

A woman, a stream,
Sunlight on a twisted path.
A man, steps behind.

SLAUGHTER

We offer as sacrifice, a goat
Stunned into two by a sword.

A ritual made real by blood;
An act to make us whole.

STONE

Your arms wrapped
around my root

My hardness folded
in your creases

Fold upon skin
stone upon flesh

Your body a shield
for all my fears

All else washes over me

My sharp edges
weathered by your grace

MEMORY

This refusal to dislodge the past:
forever her face in repose,
before any animation or sound;
as if held in a vaselined lens.

MADRAS

I have grown accustomed to this drought,
learning to live and breathe a humid air.
The rains have failed another year;
verandahs are dry, the stench chokes.

Shoving past stares and persistent guides,
I watch a row of insubstantial stalls.
A line of open sewer ferments
a step in front of vendors' huts.

A *paan* seller comes out from behind
a curtain's shade, stretches,
scratches, then in open view pisses
a step in front into the ditch.

Like fostering a fascination
with the smell of your own farts,
you add to the spill and pelt
and call it your own.

WORSHIP

He said to her, by way of example,
"Listen, when you go to your temple,
  Do not, like others here, stand
  And offer prayers with pressed hands.
  Rather, look at the images cut
  Out of stone, with your eyes shut."

ACKNOWLEDGEMENTS

For some of the poems in the *What You Left Behind* sequence, I am indebted to *Hindu Funeral Rites*, a pamphlet published by the National Council of Hindu Temples (UK), for an explanation of the procedures for cremating the dead in this country.

I am grateful to East Midlands Arts for the award of a major Writers Bursary in 1991 that enabled me to revisit India and to work on the new poems.

A number of the poems in the *Possessions* sequence were originally published in *Shadows of my Making* in 1986 by Lokamaya Press (London) in different versions with illustrations by Michael Darling.

Acknowledgements are due to the editors of *The Observer, Poetry Review, Bazaar, Other Poetry, Kunapipi, South Asian Literature in the Secondary School, Multi-cultural Teaching, Wasafiri* and *World Parnassus of Poets* (India) in which some of these poems appeared. Some poems were also broadcast on BBC and commercial radio. For permission to quote from George Barker's poem *To my Mother* from *Collected Poems 1933-1955*, acknowledgements are due to Faber and Faber. The quotations from Franz Kafka's *Letter to His Father* are translations by Ernst Kaiser and Eithne Wilkins first published in Great Britain by Martin Secker & Warburg (1954). The V.S. Naipaul quotation is from *The Enigma of Arrival* first published by Viking (1987).

On a personal note, an overdue acknowledgement to Fiona Cownie, Suresh Chauhan and particularly to Tony Bradney for criticism and persistent encouragement.

Mahendra Solanki was born in 1956 in Nairobi of Indian parents. His first collection of poems, *Shadows of my Making* was published in 1986.